GRADE 1
PIANO

12 Pieces Plus Exercises for
Trinity College London Exams
from 2023

Published by
Trinity College London Press Ltd
trinitycollege.com
Registered in England
Company no. 09726123

Copyright © 2023 Trinity College London Press Ltd
Second impression, October 2025

Unauthorised photocopying is illegal
No part of this publication may be copied or reproduced in any
form or by any means without the prior permission of the publisher.

Cover artwork: Rod Steele
Printed in England by Caligraving Ltd

Performance notes

Melodie / Vaňhal — Page 6

- Classical duet
- Contrasted articulation between hands
- Phrased three-time

During the second half of the 18th century, Vaňhal's music was much admired in Vienna and was widely published in his lifetime. Having been born into a family of bonded servants in rural Bohemia, his abilities as a musician enabled him to earn a good living and buy his freedom. He knew Haydn and Mozart and was witnessed playing string quartets with them, along with Carl Dittersdorf, a fellow composer. What an experience that must have been!

This piece is to be played with a strict pulse, but also with a sense of fun. The swing of the three-time should not be challenged by heaviness on every crotchet in the left hand. Making sure of *staccato* in the left and smooth quavers in the right can be eased into by tapping the left hand rhythms to start with.

The echo of the repeat can be very effective; practising bars 7&8 and then back to bars 1&2 with the partner can ensure that the ensemble is precise. The second half (from bar 9) begins with a short sequence of two-bar phrases. Shaping towards the stressed crotchet and away from it could colour this more intimate section well. The ending is triumphant.

Being called melody, this piece would lend itself to being sung, so it would be fun to make up some words. The music dictates where the natural stresses are, so let that form the basis for the choice of words. Which bars could perhaps use 'I played with Carl Dittersdorf, Mozart and Haydn as well'? (LN)

Water Sprite / Goodrich — Page 8

- Romantic
- ABA form
- Octave displacement

Florence Ada Goodrich was a composer and music teacher from America. Goodrich loved creating beautiful music, especially for children who were learning to play the piano. She wrote lots of fun and exciting pieces for students of different levels and abilities.

'Water Sprite' uses an ABA (ternary) form and the octave displacement (transposing) technique. Don't worry about these complex words!

In music, there's a special way to organise a song or a piece called ABA form, which is like a musical sandwich! Imagine you have a sandwich with different yummy fillings. In ABA form, the piece starts with the first section, that's the 'A' part, like the first slice of bread. Then comes the 'B' section, which is like the tasty filling in the middle. It sounds a bit different from the 'A' section, maybe with new notes or a different melody.

Finally, the song goes back to the 'A' section, like the second slice of bread, to finish the sandwich. This helps the song feel complete and balanced.

In 'Water Sprite' Florence uses this technique very cleverly — see if you can spot the ABA form here, it's not easy to spot straight-away (the secret is in the 'D.C. al Fine' instruction at the end of the 2nd page).

The octave displacement technique is very simple — it is using the same set of notes or a phrase and transposing it up or down an octave. If that sounds complicated, think of it like a game of moving up or down on a magical staircase! Imagine you have a special tune or a set of notes that you really like. Octave displacement lets you take that tune and move it up or down on the musical staircase, so it sounds higher or lower. It's a bit like playing on different steps of a ladder! By using octave displacement, composers can create new versions of melodies or patterns and make the music sound more interesting. See if you can spot the octave displacement technique in bars 1&3 and in bars 9&11. (YC)

Chris's Song (from *Very Easy Piano Pieces for Children*, op. 3) / Garścia — Page 10

- 20th century
- Right-hand tune
- Articulation

Janina Garścia was a Polish composer, pianist and teacher who wrote around 700 pieces, mostly for children. 'Chris's Song' is a beautiful but simple example of her writing.

This piece consists of a song-like melody in the right hand with a simple accompaniment consisting of minims in the left hand. The first eight bars of the piece are in the key of A minor and have a feeling of sadness, which you can bring to life by making the most of the hairpins (*crescendos* and *diminuendos*). Make sure to distinguish the *legato* and *staccato* elements of this tune and really connect the *legato* passages together with your fingers to bring the melody out. The middle section is happier: we move to the key of C major for eight bars, notice the strong dynamic contrasts between *forte* and *piano*. Then the opening idea returns, but make sure to be quieter than at the start.

Is this piece depicting the moods of a friend called Chris who is sometimes sad and sometimes happy? It might help to imagine the music is written as a description of a real person, in order to make your performance even more engaging. (WV)

Hug a Pug / Arens — Page 12

- Jazzy
- Swing rhythm
- Ostinato in the left hand

'Hug a Pug' is a super fun and catchy piece that will make you want to dance and sing along! It's all about the adorable and cuddly pugs, those squishy-faced dogs with wagging tails. The melody is bouncy and lively, and the lyrics are all about how pugs make us happy and bring smiles to our faces.

The swing rhythm, is a special way of playing music that makes you want to tap your feet and dance along, it's like a musical bounce! Instead of playing the notes equally, like a steady drum, swing rhythm makes some notes longer and some shorter. This is also shown at the start of the piece after the metronome marking. You could have a listen to a recording of songs from 'The Jungle Book' which are in a swing rhythm, such as 'I Wan'na Be Like You', or 'Baloo's Blues'.

Ostinato is a musical word that means having a repeating pattern, like a musical rhythm that keeps coming back again and again. It could be a short melody, a rhythmic pattern, or even a chord progression that stays the same while other elements of the music change. The word ostinato comes from the Italian word 'ostinare', which means 'to persist' or 'to be stubborn'. Just like a catchy rhythm or melody that sticks in your head, an ostinato persists and repeats to create a foundation for the rest of the music. (YC)

A Peculiar Party / Li — Page 13

- New commission
- Atmospheric
- Contrast of articulation between hands

Zhenyan Li is a Chinese composer based in London. She likes to write music which takes inspiration from the theatre, but especially traditional Chinese theatre, so don't be surprised to hear some quite dramatic moments in 'A Peculiar Party'!

What do you like to have at a traditional party? Some of the first things which spring to mind are clowns, balloons, magicians, and jelly and ice cream. But at THIS party almost everything is a surprise, and may sound unexpected to you…

The right-hand notes at the beginning clash together, so we know from the start that things aren't what we might normally expect. The *staccatos* also help add to the atmosphere here – spooky, hushed, mysterious – is everybody hiding and waiting? What mood do you think the first two little left-hand snippets of tune are trying to conjure up, especially with the dramatic *crescendo* in bars 3 and 4? Has everyone just jumped out to surprise you? You can really enjoy all the surprises in this piece, because you get to play both the softest and loudest sounds that your piano can make!

Playing smoothly in one hand and detached in the other can be a challenge at first. You may want to start with just one note in each hand at a time, then moving on to some simple 5-finger exercises, playing slowly up and down with *staccato* in one hand and *legato* in the other, and then swapping over after a few attempts. (DB)

Railbird Rag / Cleaver — Page 14

- Ragtime
- Differing articulations
- Counting rests accurately

The *staccato* notes are easy-going, nothing too extreme or pointed. A general buoyant *legato* in the treble will contrast well with the left hand, although slurs are implied over the 2nd and 3rd, 4th and 5th melody notes in bar 17.

The pulse must be constant and this is particularly important in the last three bars. To accurately place the notes here, you could practise filling the space with something: words, snippets of music from elsewhere in the piece, or even taps on the wood of the piano. Rests should have positive energy; they are seldom just empty space but places where the tension can dissipate from the previous notes or even increase.

Here the ending is cheeky, it should make us smile; it is so understated after the busy, restless nature of the rest of the piece. Just like an casual lift of the hat as you leave the stage. (PL/MR)

103 East 86th Street (from *She Stoops to Conquer*) / Ringham/Ringham — Page 16

- Waltz
- Contrasting articulations between the hands
- Dynamic changes

Composers Ben and Max Ringham have collaborated on music for theatre, film and TV for over 20 years. This piece is taken from a 2012 stage production at the National Theatre of the 1773 Oliver Goldsmith period comedy *She Stoops to Conquer*.

The tempo marking for this is a *Lilting waltz*. This music is best performed with a strong sense of rhythm and purpose – imagine a dance floor filled with swirling couples in old-fashioned outfits!

The left hand has a regular 'oom-cha-cha' figure in which the slurs and dynamics help to achieve the right sense of momentum and grace. Meanwhile, the right had has contrasting *legato* material. You might like to work on these different approaches one hand at a time to begin with.

In giving a good performance of this piece, it is important to pay attention to the rests in the melody line (for example bar 5, beat 3 and elsewhere).

It's fun to make the most of the *crescendos* and *diminuendos* within each phrase, and of course the sudden *forte* dynamic marking at bar 21. This moment is full of drama and surprise, as though the dance floor has turned to lava, as the music winds down.

Waltzes are a common form for compositions and it's a good idea to listen to a few to embed the style. The Strauss family was notable for composing many waltzes. Every New Year's Day the Vienna Philharmonic perform a concert programme full of Strauss compositions which is broadcast worldwide. Perhaps the most famous is the 'The Blue Danube' composed by Johann Strauss II. (PE)

The Music Box / Moore Page 18

- Contemporary character piece
- Playing an octave higher in both hands
- Singing melody over active accompaniment

This sweet piece conjures an image of a mechanical music box. Imagining what it looks like would be a way of communicating this. Is anything sitting on the top, turning around? Is it old-fashioned?

The left hand has an alberti pattern, characterising the motion of the mechanics of the box. Practising holding your thumb in a relaxed way on the G or A key and only playing the moving bass notes helps to keep this comfortable as well as not drowning out the right hand.

The melody needs to sing out, with deep tone. Finding a shape for each phrase brings the music to life; is the first note the most important, or is there a high point elsewhere? Shifting up the octave requires careful placing of the hands, so practising bars 8 and 9 several times makes this movement reliable. Actually, practising from one first beat to the next a few times for each bar is a way of keeping the music flowing. At the end, there is a *molto rit*. What could this mean?

Finding out about how a music box works would be interesting, as would listening to some. They come in all shapes and sizes and their melodies vary very much. (LN)

Titanium (Sia and David Guetta) /
Furler/Guetta/Tuinfort/van de Wall *arr.* Hussey Page 20

- Pop
- Drum emulation
- Steady pulse

This song features on the album *Nothing but the Beat* by French DJ and record producer David Guetta.

The tempo instruction 'with a driving beat' at the start of the piece acknowledges the energetic 'house' style of the original recording.

The piece starts with a *mf* dynamic; there should be a sense of intensity and anticipation, but take care not to start too loudly. In bar 9 the dynamic is *f* and the accompaniment is more rhythmic, resembling the 'four-on-the-floor' bass drum associated with this genre.

A *crescendo* starts the build into the climax in bar 17, with the now 'thumping' bass drum represented by the *staccato* left hand against off-beat quavers in the right.

It's perhaps worth noting that, at this point the music video, a cyclist is featured pedalling as fast as they can!

Take care to maintain a steady pulse throughout, resisting any temptation to speed up when the energy intensifies (and not to slow down at the end...) (MR)

Grumpy Gorilla / Arens Page 22

- Blues
- Articulation; *staccato* and accents
- Crossing hands

Composer Barbara Arens began her studies aged 13 and went on to have a performance career as a harpsichordist and organist. She is a passionately dedicated piano teacher and has composed a wealth of new music tailored to her piano students.

In this piece the *staccato* left hand boogie-woogie accompaniment sounds like the heavy grunts of the Gorilla! The form of this piece is a 12-bar blues. This is a hugely influential sound that developed from the African-American tradition of music-making in the 19th century and would lead to the development of Jazz, Rock & Roll and countless other musical art forms.

This piece sounds best performed with a consistent pulse and groove – it doesn't want to speed up or slow down (until the marked *rit.* at the end). The left hand is almost entirely *staccato* throughout, meanwhile the right hand is more *legato*, including accents and bluesy acciaccaturas (also known as crushed notes). It's fun to make the most of the *fortissimo* dynamic in bar 11 onwards, but don't forget the *diminuendo* in the final two bars!

In the final bar the left hand crosses over to higher up the keyboard than the right hand and plays a three-note chord with a pause. You might like to rehearse this movement slowly and pay attention to where the left hand is headed before depressing the keys.

For further studies, there are numerous left-hand and right-hand boogie-woogie patterns that build on the movement learned in this piece. You could have a listen to some recordings by famous boogie-woogie pianists, such as Fats Domino and Chuck Berry. (PE)

God Bless the Child (Billie Holiday) /
Holiday/ Herzog Jr. *arr.* Vicari Page 24

- Jazz ballad
- Swing feel
- Blues harmonies

Billie Holiday was a jazz singer who wrote this song in the 1940s, when jazz was a popular music. There is a soulful, sad quality to this composition and the use of the major and minor 3rd (used in blues) shapes its mood.

There are many typical jazz elements in this piece such as the swinging syncopated rhythm in the left-hand pattern in the first five bars. Playing with a relaxed hand and a strong swung quaver feel will make the music really flow and sound jazzy! The right hand carries the melody and will need to be louder than the left hand but still be aware of the overall dynamics.

There are some lovely jazz harmonies in bars 7 and 8 in the right hand – aim to 'bounce' on the chords with a gentle touch.

In jazz music, the double bass often plays a scale-like pattern called a 'walking bass' and we see this in the left hand in bar 9. The two hands at this point move independently and require careful coordination. We get a real sense that the music is coming to an end when the initial pattern returns. Aim to maintain the tempo until the last few notes marked *rit.* (slow down) to bring the music to a close.

Suggested listening: 'God Bless the Child' by Billie Holiday.   (AV)

Guajira Guantanamera (aka Guantanamera) /
Diaz *arr.* Wilson   Page 25

- Latin
- Cuban rhythm
- Song

Music from Cuba often has an underlying pulse called a clave and this drives and frames the groove. Guantanamera is a Cuban folksong.

This arrangement has a short introduction followed by an 8-bar melody. Dotted rhythms in the left hand and a repeated phrase in the right sets the scene. When the melody begins (bar 5) we are right there in Cuba with the words 'Guan-tan-a-mera' providing the rhythm of the tune, make sure that you give prominence to the right-hand melody. Playing with a firm *legato* touch and a bounce on repeated notes will lift the music. The left hand is repetitive in rhythm although the pitches are varied, mostly outlining chord shapes. Clapping the various rhythms of both hands first, will get you familiar with the groove.

The final chord is spread from the bottom note upwards with a gentle feel, avoiding any tension in the hand, to end the music with style and a slight slowing up! (AV)

Authors:

- Daniel Beach (DB)
- Yulia Chaplina (YC)
- Gregory Drott (GD)
- Paul Edis (PE)
- John Human (JH)
- Pamela Lidiard/Michael Round (PL/MR)
- Linda Nottingham (LN)
- Matthew Regan (MR)
- William Vann (WV)
- Andrea Vicari (AV)

Melodie
(duet part)

Jan Křtitel Vaňhal
1739-1813

In the exam do observe the repeat

Copyright © 2023 Trinity College London Press Ltd

Melodie

(candidate's part)

Jan Křtitel Vaňhal
1739-1813

In the exam do observe the repeat

Water Sprite

Florence Ada Goodrich
1850-1928

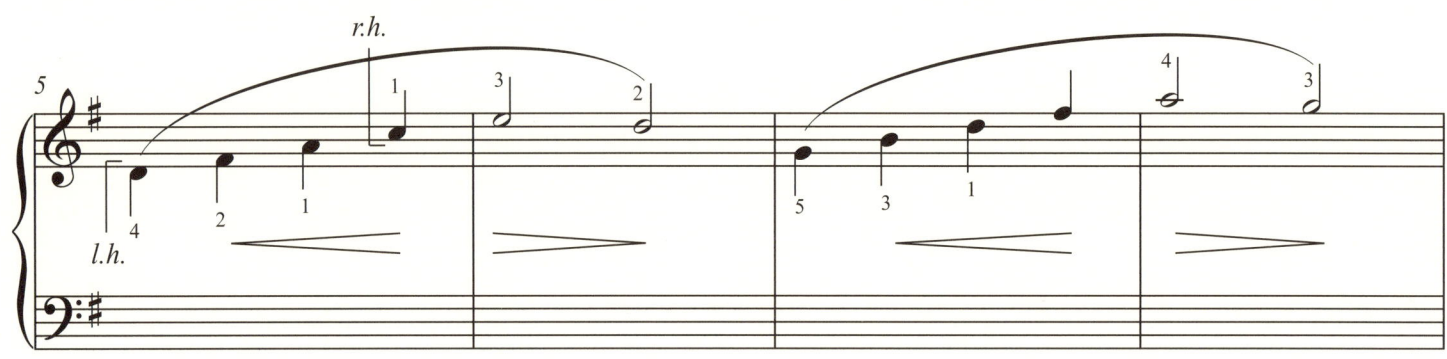
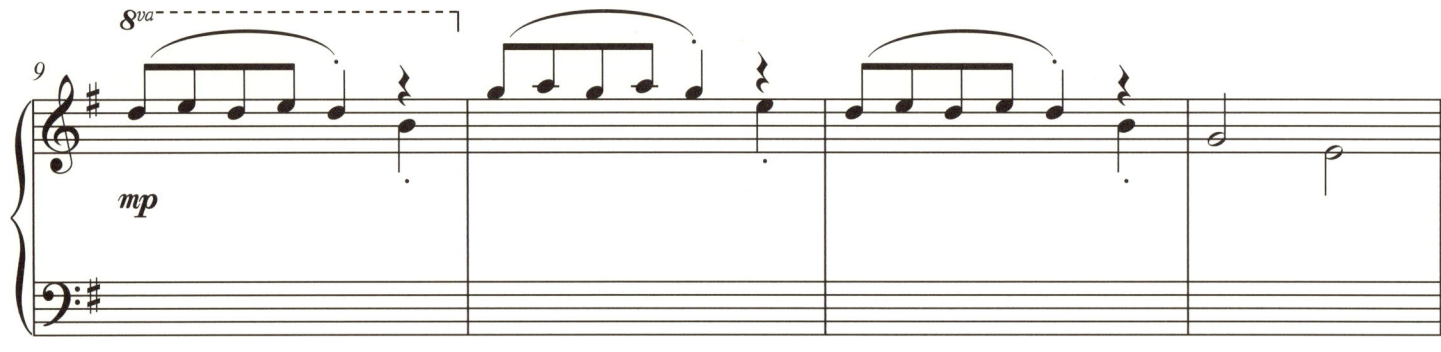
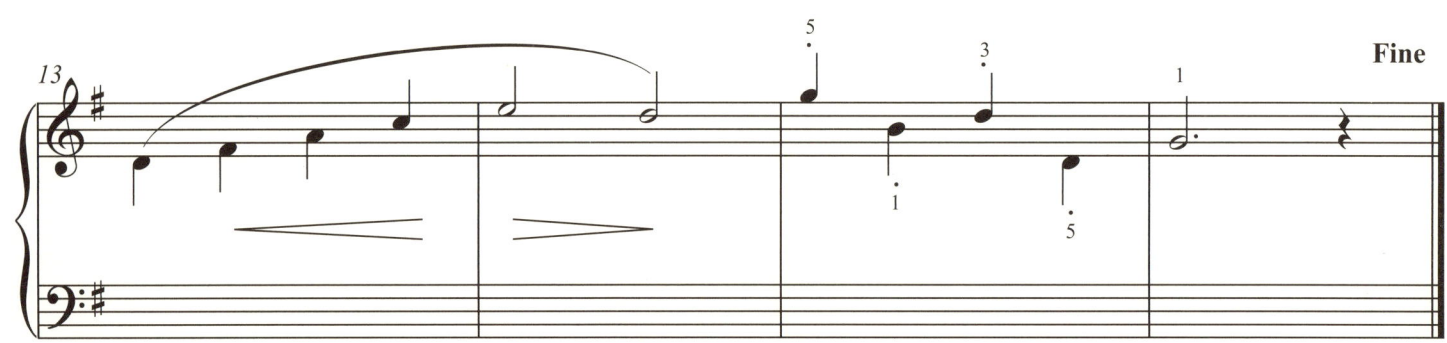

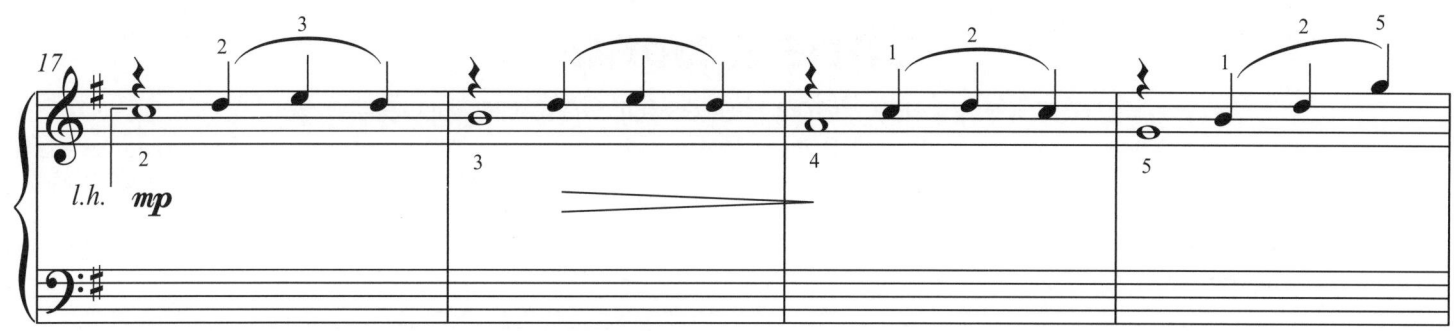
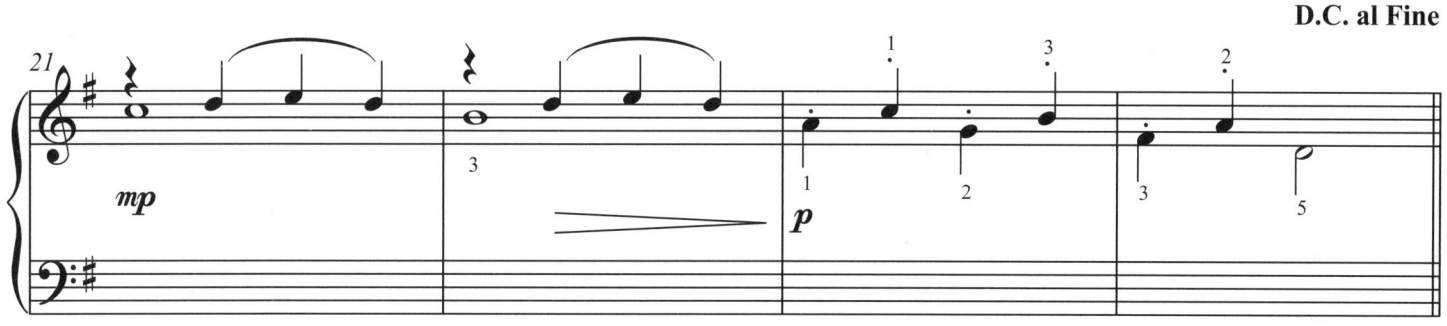

Chris's Song
from *Very Easy Piano Pieces for Children*, op. 3

Janina Garścia
1920-2004

Hug a Pug

Barbara Arens
b. 1960

From: *Chubby Hippo & Friends - 10 Really Easy Piano Pieces with Really Silly Lyrics.*
Copyright © 2018 Barbara Arens. All rights reserved

A Peculiar Party

Zhenyan Li
b. 1998

Railbird Rag

Sam Cleaver
b. 1982

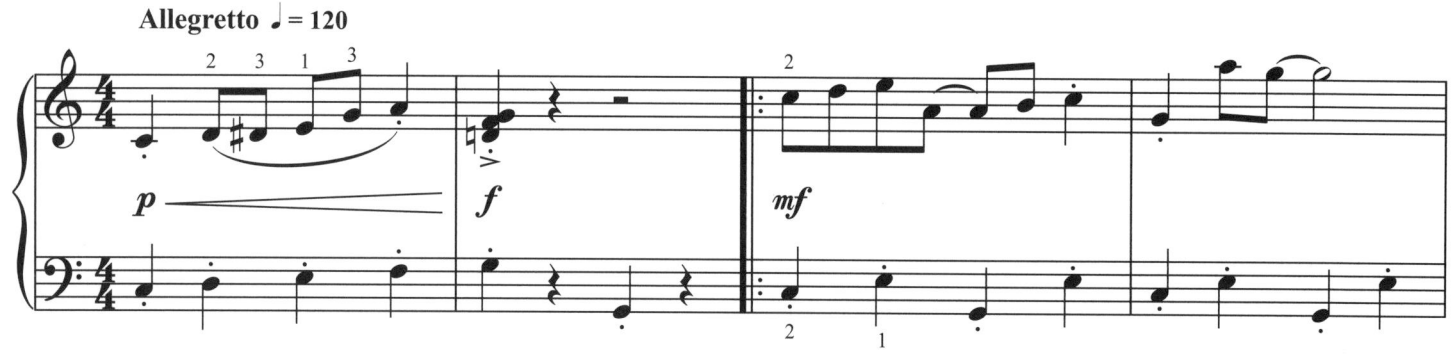

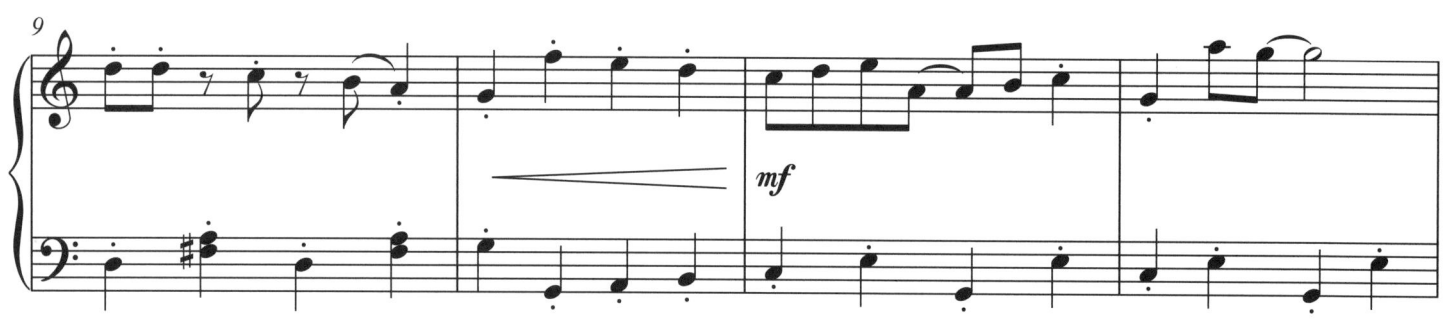
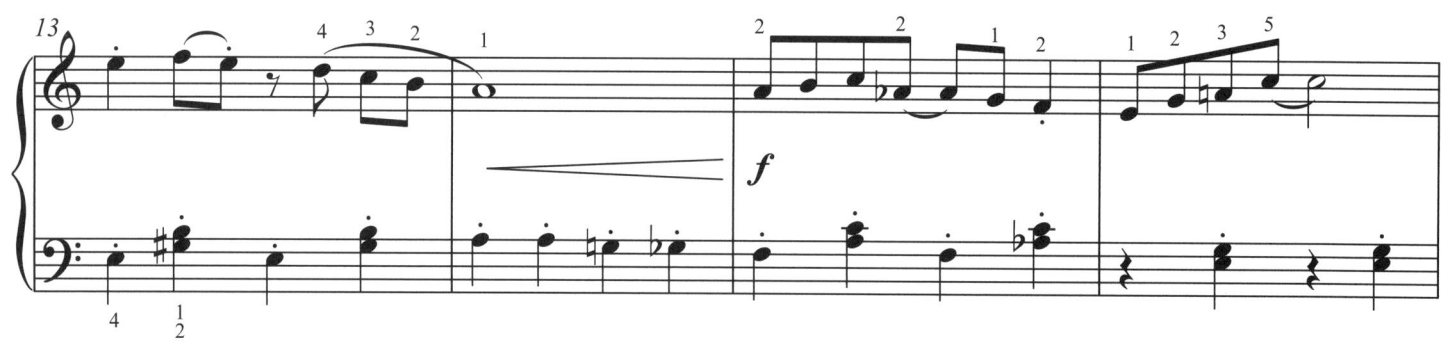

In the exam omit the repeat

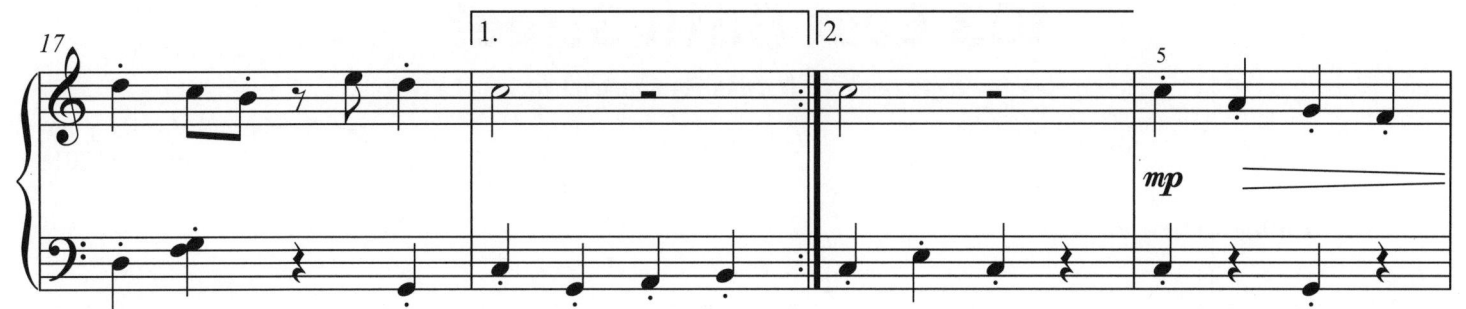
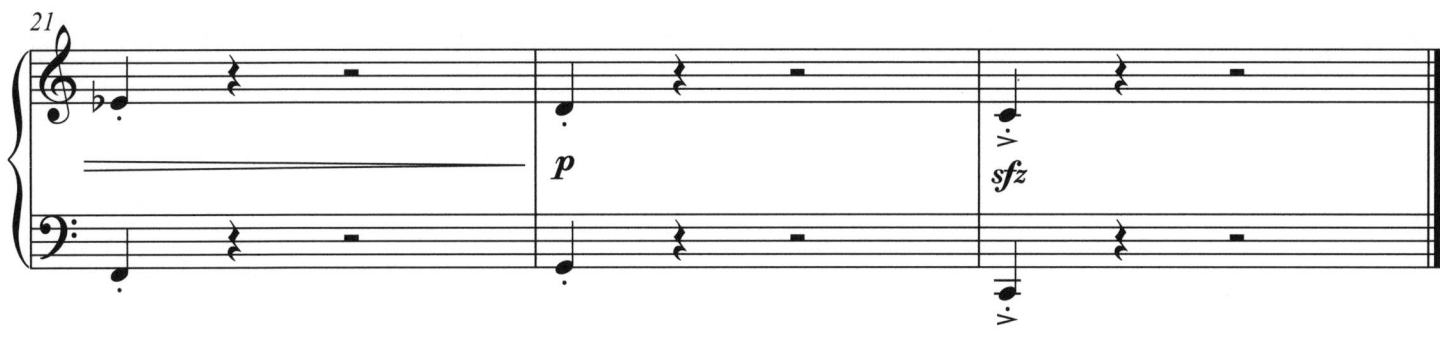

103 East 86th Street

from *She Stoops to Conquer*

Ben Ringham & Max Ringham
released 2012

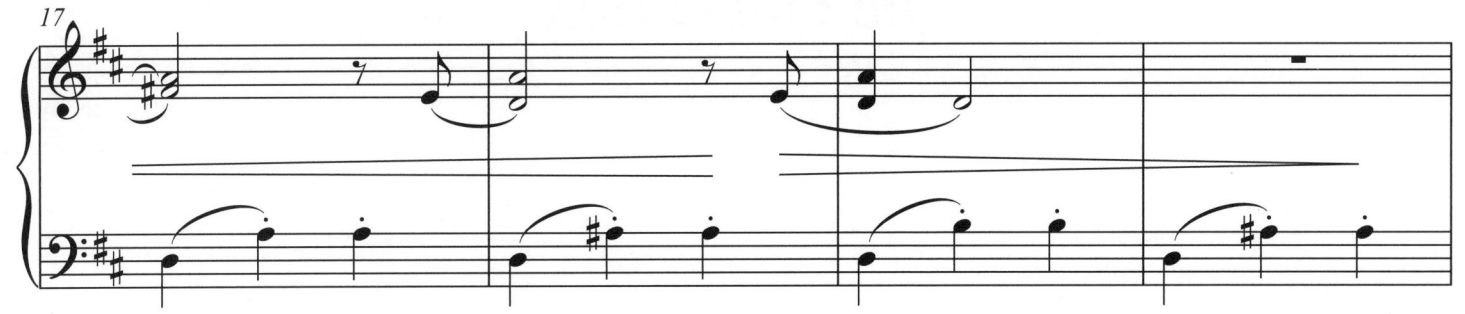

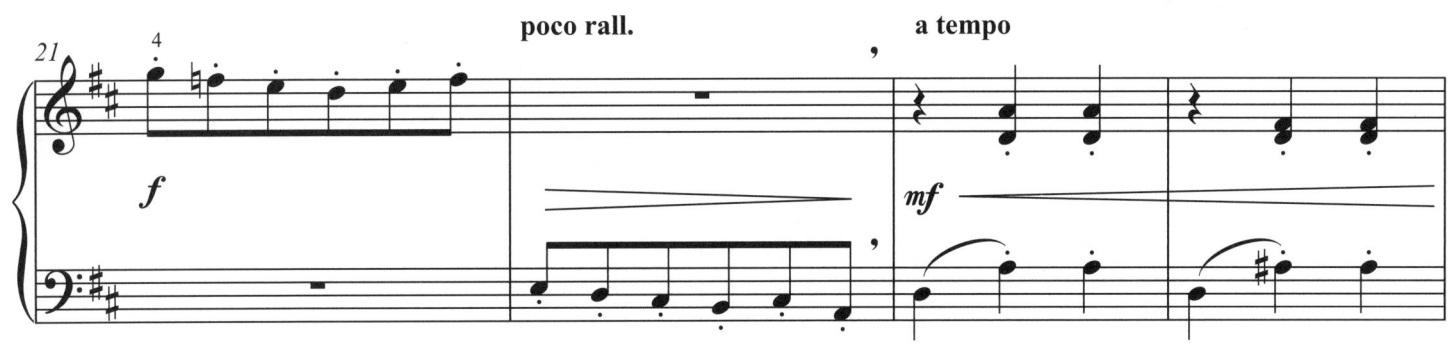

The Music Box

Ray Moore
b. 1939

Titanium
(Sia and David Guetta)

Sia Furler, David Guetta,
Giorgio Tuinfort & Nick van de Wall
released 2011
arr. Chris Hussey

With a driving beat ♩ = 116

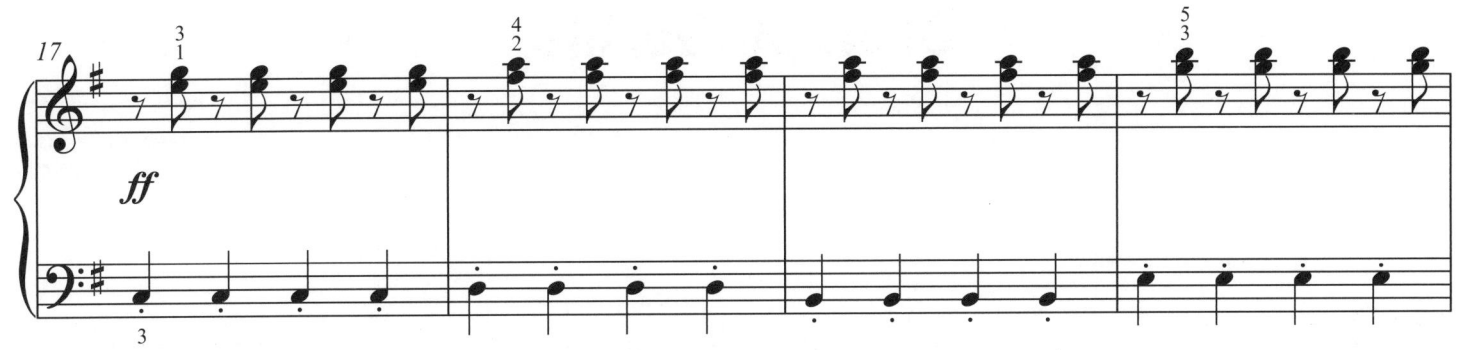
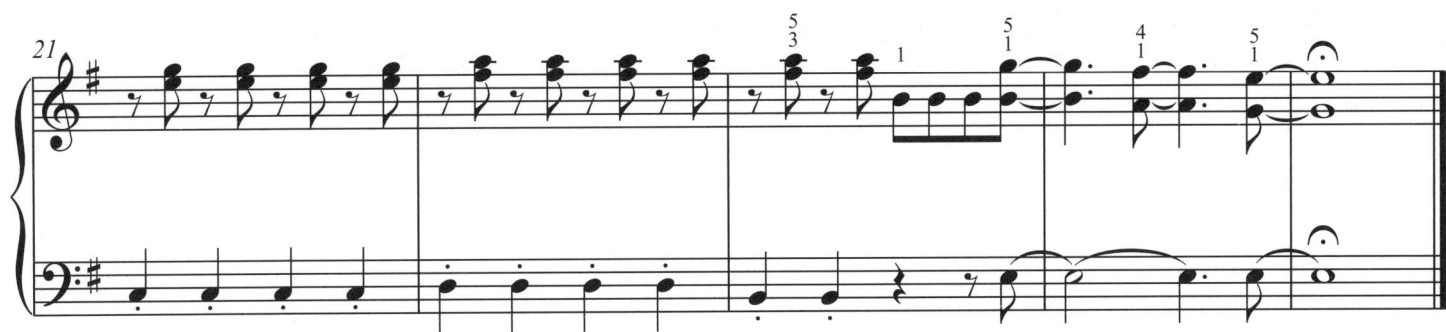

Grumpy Gorilla

Barbara Arens
b. 1960

From: *Chubby Hippo & Friends - 10 Really Easy Piano Pieces with Really Silly Lyrics*.
Copyright © 2018 Barbara Arens. All rights reserved

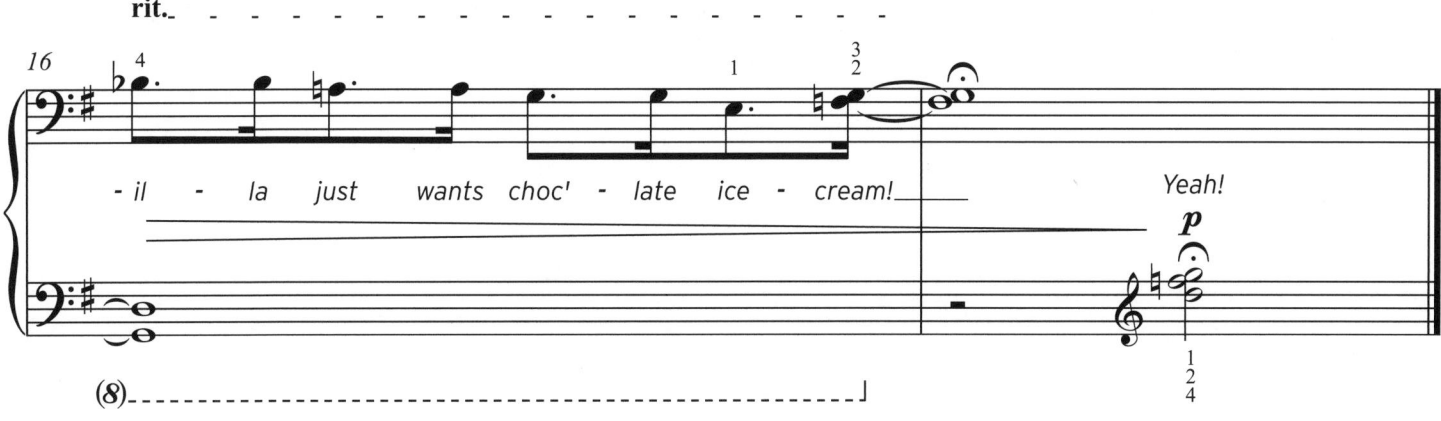

God Bless the Child
(Billie Holiday)

Billie Holiday & Arthur Herzog Jr.
released 1942
arr. Andrea Vicari

© 1941 Edward B. Marks Music Company. All rights reserved.
Used by kind permission of Carlin Music Delaware LLC,
Clearwater Yard, 35 Inverness Street, London, NW1 7HB.

Guajira Guantanamera
(aka Guantanamera)

José Fernández Diaz
released 1929
arr. Alex Wilson

Exercises

Candidates may select from the exercises below, or from the 2021 books (labelled 1a, 1b etc), or a mixture of the two. Please refer to the syllabus for further information.

1c. Wanderer – tone, balance and voicing

1d. Stepladder – tone, balance and voicing

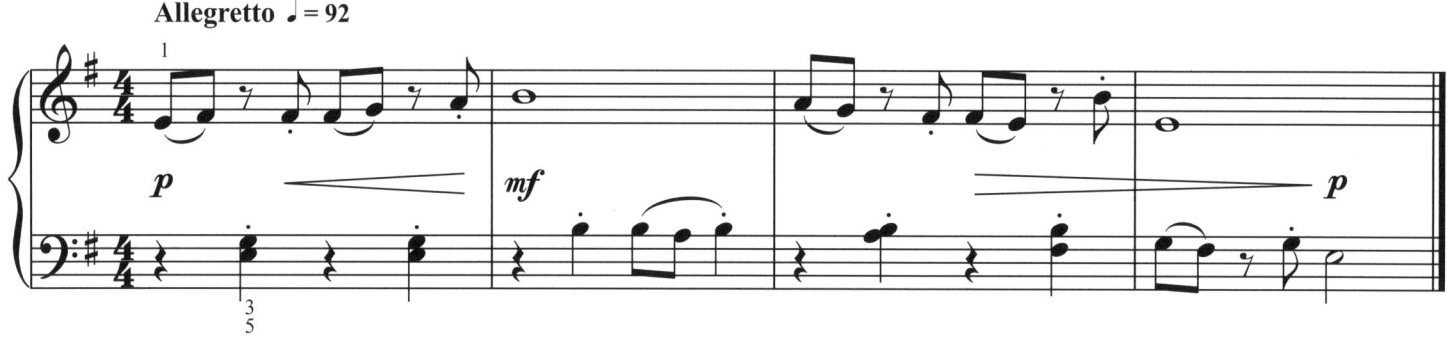

2c. Ironing Out – co-ordination

2d. Footsteps – co-ordination

3c. Echo Chamber – finger & wrist strength and flexibility

3d. Snakes and Ladders – finger & wrist strength and flexibility

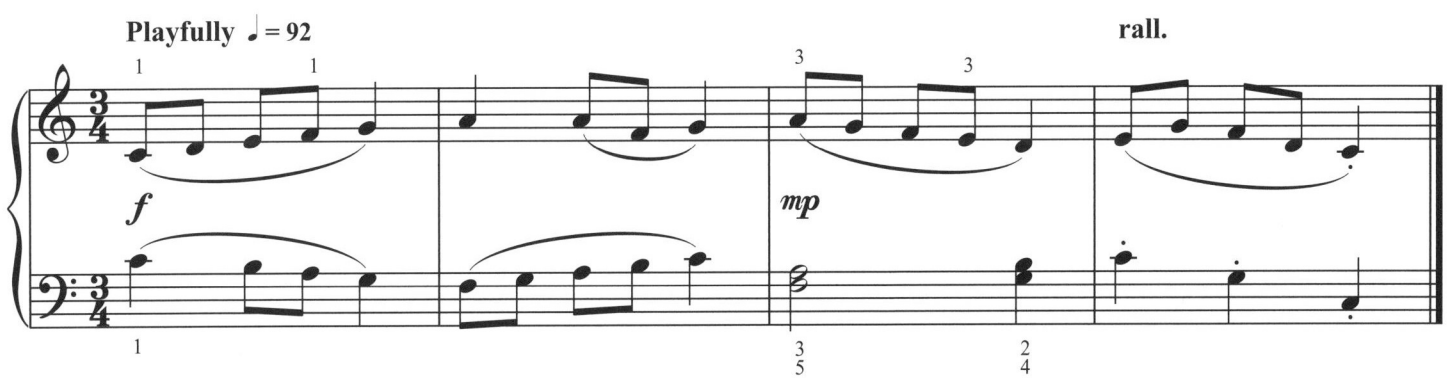